'*Come Closer* helps you ⟨barcode⟩ strategies you didn't know, , what to do with. Sand gets them out in the open where she shows you how to dismantle them, one by one, and allow yourself to become rooted, instead, in security, self-acceptance and love.'

— *Deborah Ward, HSP and Personal Growth Writer*

'As a sex and relationship therapist, I was moved and captivated by this exquisite book. Every page spoke to me. It is beautifully written, using helpful examples to illustrate each point. It made me think about how to deepen relationships in ways that I had never considered before, and I have been a couples' therapist for 25 years! A brilliant book that will help you to be closer to yourself, your lived reality, and thus to others. An absolute "must-read" for anyone who wants more from intimate relationships. I can think of hundreds of people who will benefit from reading this book.'

— *Juliet Grayson, UKCP Registered Psychosexual Therapist and author of* Landscapes of the Heart

COME CLOSER

by the same author

Highly Sensitive People in an Insensitive World
How to Create a Happy Life
ISBN 978 1 78592 066 0
eISBN 978 1 78450 324 6

The Emotional Compass
How to Think Better about Your Feelings
ISBN 978 1 78592 127 8
eISBN 978 1 78450 392 5

Tools for Helpful Souls
ISBN 978 1 78592 296 1
eISBN 978 1 78450 599 8

COME CLOSER

On Love and Self-Protection

ILSE SAND

Jessica Kingsley *Publishers*
London and Philadelphia

First published by Forlaget Ammentorp, Denmark in 2014

English language edition first published in 2017
by Jessica Kingsley Publishers
73 Collier Street
London N1 9BE, UK
and
400 Market Street, Suite 400
Philadelphia, PA 19106, USA

www.jkp.com

Copyright © Ilse Sand 2017

English language edition translated by Russell Dees

Library of Congress Cataloging in Publication Data
Names: Sand, Ilse, author.
Title: Come closer : on love and self-protection / Ilse Sand.
Description: London ; Philadelphia : Jessica Kingsley Publishers, 2017. |
    Includes bibliographical references.
Identifiers: LCCN 2017013113 (print) | LCCN 2016054757 (ebook) | ISBN
    9781784506032 (ebook) | ISBN 9781785922978 (alk. paper)
Subjects: LCSH: Self-protective behavior. | Interpersonal relations. |
    Intimacy (Psychology)
Classification: LCC BF697.5.S45 (print) | LCC BF697.5.S45 S26 2017 (ebook) |
    DDC 158.2--dc23

British Library Cataloguing in Publication Data
A CIP catalogue record for this book is available from the British Library

ISBN 978 1 78592 297 8
eISBN 978 1 78450 603 2

Printed and bound in the United States

CONTENTS

PREFACE

In my time as a pastor and, later, as a psychotherapist, I have talked to many people who have been hurt by love – if they have been lucky enough to find someone to love.

I have learned in connection with my lectures on love and self-protection that there is great interest in becoming wiser about the psychological mechanisms at play in our relationships – both when we form them and in their everyday interactions.

In this book, I describe how self-protection strategies arise, how they can stand in the way of good, close relationships, and how undesirable strategies can be dismantled.

I have learned how relationships can become deeper and more meaningful if we dare to be fully present in the moment in all our vulnerability, shed of unnecessary armour.

The literature on this topic in which I have steeped myself was written for professionals. However, the present book is written in more accessible language that can be read by anyone. At the same time, it is solidly anchored in recognised psychological theories and many years of therapeutic experience.

The many specific examples in the book are, for the most part, invented for instructive purposes but contain situations and remarks I often encounter in my practice. Some of the examples are authentic and retold anonymously with permission from the relevant client.

It is my hope that this knowledge, which I have seen make a difference for clients and myself, will benefit a much wider audience far beyond those who read the professional literature or are in treatment.

INTRODUCTION

Why don't we all live in vibrant, loving relationships with other people? Why do so many people live alone or in relationships that lack closeness and a genuine concern for one another?

There may be different answers to this. One of them is that we use self-protection strategies to trick ourselves and trip ourselves up in love.

Anyone who works in psychotherapy is familiar with self-protection strategies. Clients use various strategies to distance themselves from other people, to avoid looking hard at their own lives, or to suppress their own inner feelings, thoughts, knowledge or desires.

These strategies have been called different things over the years. Freud called them 'defence mechanisms' (*abwerf*). Cognitive therapy works with the concept of 'coping strategies', which sometimes describes the same observations.

Even Søren Kierkegaard, who formulated his ideas more than half a century before Freud, noticed the phenomenon. He wrote that human beings have a peculiar ability to muddle up their own knowledge (Kierkegaard 1989). How they actually do that Kierkegaard did not dwell on. We know more about it today.

I have chosen to call these manoeuvres – through which we sometimes muddle up the most obvious things or keep other people and our own inner selves at a distance – 'self-protection strategies'. By this, I mean everything a human being does (consciously or, more often, unconsciously) to avoid closeness with other people or his or her own internal or external reality.

Self-protection may also entail such things as quitting smoking or putting on a lifejacket while at sea. The self-protection strategies in which I am interested in this book, however, are those we use to distance ourselves from reality. Sometimes, this may be advantageous. At other times, it may become a problem.

Self-protection is good if it allows you to distance yourself from your feelings when they become overwhelming. But this same self-protection strategy can become a problem if it is inflexible and allowed unconsciously (either entirely or only partially) to take on a life of its own.

Our quality of life and our vitality are affected when we create more distance to our inner lives than is necessary. And when we distance ourselves from the realities of our actual life situation, we do not see them clearly, and our lives become difficult to navigate.

One self-protection strategy, for example, may be using your imagination to reshape external reality, so you see yourself, other people or your opportunities as better or worse than they realistically are. Another, more concrete example may be when you fail to breathe deeply enough really to feel yourself.

A self-protection strategy is a tactic that was once a shrewd solution to a difficult situation. If you needed to resort to many self-protection strategies in childhood, you may find yourself as an adult so wrapped up in your own self-protection that it is impossible to achieve good emotional contact with yourself or others. And, in this way, you may miss out on the inner blossoming that a loving connection can awaken.

It is my hope that this book will stimulate you as a reader to look at your own self-protection strategies and to consider whether your life might become richer if you abandoned one or more of them, so you can get closer to yourself, to your life and to other people – and get more enjoyment out of your life while you are here.

Chapter 1

SELF-PROTECTION STRATEGIES

The self-protection strategies in which I am interested in this book are manoeuvres we use to distance ourselves from our inner lives, from other people and from the external realities of our life. From now on, this is what I mean when I use the term 'self-protection strategy'.

A concrete example of a self-protection strategy may be the following. Hannah has had a job application rejected. She is sad but does not have the energy to feel her sorrow right here and now. She chooses instead to watch a thriller on TV and forget herself. In this way, she gives herself a break from the reality in which she finds herself after a job rejection.

This is not a problem as long as she gives herself the time and the space later to feel and grapple with her sorrow and, thus, become fully present again. However, if it is the only strategy she uses to deal with difficult feelings, if she never gives herself the time and space to relax and feel what she is feeling, it is a problem. She will live with a permanent distance to herself, and this may cause emotional stress or a lack of genuine vitality. If she does not realise that she is creating a distance to her feelings, it becomes an even greater problem because she will have no opportunity to alter this behaviour.

Most self-protection strategies arise early in childhood. At that time, they were the best solution a small child could find to a difficult situation. Later, self-protection strategies can become unconscious and engage automatically each time we find ourselves in a situation that resembles one of the unresolved crises of our childhood.

A concrete example may illustrate this. Iris's mother was often depressed and spoke about her pain when Iris was growing up. It was unbearable for Iris to listen to. A child cannot handle an adult's despair, and it is also terrifying to know that your caregiver is having a hard time. So, when she was quite small, Iris developed a strategy in these situations of changing the subject entirely in order to distract her mother and to get her to think about something else.

Today, she wonders why her children do not come to her with their troubles. If she asks them why, they usually say that they have tried but that all their attempts end up with their mother talking about something else.

If Iris had recorded one of their conversations, she would probably be able to hear how – without knowing it – she changes the subject each time she feels or hears about the crisis or sorrow of someone close to her.

It is, of course, destructive to closeness in relationships if we resort to such self-protection strategies without being aware of it.

If Iris can recognise and see her own pattern, which may have once saved her psychological well-being but, today, stands in the way of intimacy with her children, she has already gone a long way towards altering her strategy.

Survival techniques

A self-protection strategy is most often a survival technique.

An example: when Anna was very small, her parents reacted negatively when she tried to get their attention. They might say she was irritating or she would see stress or discomfort in their eyes. It was so unpleasant for her that she gave up and went out into life without developing and learning what we might call a healthy 'asking for attention' skill.

Instead, she used all her creativity to find another solution, for children are deeply dependent on having a close attachment to a caregiver. She discovered that, if she offered them her attention instead, things went better. So, when she felt a desire for attention, she would sit down beside her newspaper-reading father and express interest in what he was reading. Most of the time, her father thought this was quite agreeable, and she could sit close to him and feel the warmth from his body and, in this way, receive the experience of connectedness on which children are vitally dependent.

As an adult, Anna has developed good skills in holding herself back and, instead, offering her attention to others, and this is a good ability to have. The problem is that she no longer feels her own need for attention very precisely. She feels an urge to be with others. When she does, she typically seeks out a girlfriend and, once they have sat down to coffee, she asks, 'How are you?' Most people are happy to be asked this, and her girlfriend talks and talks. Yet Anna cannot understand why she becomes more and more irritated and frustrated.

Without being aware of it herself, she is using a survival technique she learned in childhood. She no longer feels her own need for attention or, as soon as she becomes conscious of it, she lets it go. Instead, the survival technique takes over.

Once Anna realises how she handles her own need for attention, she can change her behaviour. The next time she sits down with a friend, she may be able to talk more about herself for a change.

And Anna's husband will be relieved when, instead of annoying him with her frustration, she tells him exactly what she wants – for example, 'I would be really happy to get your undivided attention for the next 15 minutes.'

This may sound simple and pain free. It is not. When Anna becomes aware of her survival technique and realises how she has neglected her own need for attention, she will experience sorrow. She may relive episodes from her childhood that were the reason she renounced her own need. When she stops resorting to this survival technique, she will feel helpless and insecure in her contact with others until she finds and learns a new way to relate to them.

Self-protection as a temporary solution

I want to tell a story that illustrates what self-protection can be and how it can be actively utilised and given up again in good, safe surroundings.

Six-year-old Jasper puts his schoolbag on his back, waves goodbye to his mother and makes his way to school. On the way, he passes a couple of bigger boys. Jasper smiles at them; but, just as he runs past, one of them sticks his foot out, so Jasper stumbles over it. He falls and hurts his knee. It is bleeding. The bigger boys laugh at him and call him a stupid little kid until they turn and leave.

Jasper's lips are quivering, and he considers for a moment turning around and running home to his mother. However, his desire to go to school and be with his friends wins out over his urge to run home. So, Jasper goes to school, but he is no longer happy. In fact, he was shocked by the boys' behaviour, and his knee hurts.

He does not feel very well at school and tries to forget the episode and concentrate on what is going on in the classroom. He distances himself from his fright and tries to keep from attending to his feelings. This becomes very hard when the teacher on playground duty, Benita, asks him, 'How are you doing, Jasper?' She tilts her head and looks at him sympathetically. Jasper feels the tears welling up but prevents himself from crying by moving away quickly, dismissing Benita. 'Good,' he calls to her as he hurries away.

Jasper tries to take part in the other children's ball game, but he does not feel any desire to play.

When Jasper comes home, his mother is not there. So, he sits down at the computer and starts playing a game. A little later, his mother comes through the door and says, 'Hi, Jasper.' At that moment, Jasper bursts into tears. Mother comes in, picks him up and puts him on her lap. They talk about the episode with the big boys and how much it hurt and how scared he got. Mother washes his knee and puts a bandage on it.

Not long afterwards, Jasper is happy again and ready to play. He is once again in touch with his emotions and feels the desire to play and have fun.

When Jasper decided to go to school after his frightening experience, he distanced himself from his feelings. All day at school, he struggled to keep his tears under control. In a way, this can be said to be a waste of one's life. During the time from when Jasper hurts his knee until he reacts to it with his mother, he is out of contact with himself and his pain – and also with his joy and desire to play. He becomes robot-like and just tries to adapt.

On the other hand, it is wise for Jasper to wait to give in to his feelings until he is in safe surroundings with his mother, who can help him deal with and understand this unpleasant experience. It is not wise to give way to his feelings just anywhere or with just anyone. If he had given way to his feelings and expressed them to Benita in the schoolyard, she might have looked at him disapprovingly and told him to pull himself together. That would have been extremely disagreeable for him, and he would have felt even worse.

What Jasper does instead, from the time he runs into the bigger boys until he is home with his mother, is to endure. He keeps his own feelings away from himself. He is mastering a self-protection strategy, and that is good. And, luckily for him, he has a mother who can console him and help him resolve his feelings and get back in touch with himself.

Using a self-protection strategy as a temporary solution is often a good idea, and it is good to be able to do it. In this way, you can control to a higher degree when to care for your inner self and when to prioritise conforming to social conventions or just focusing on the tasks or challenges you are facing at the moment.

How you can protect yourself both externally and internally

Two forms of self-protection may be distinguished. One form protects you against feeling your own frightening emotions, thoughts or desires. This is called intrapsychic self-protection. The second protects you against others coming too close. This is interpersonal self-protection. It comes between you and others.

Jasper uses both intrapsychic and interpersonal self-protection strategies. For one thing, he distances himself from his feelings. He straightens up and takes a breath or two. And, for another, he distances himself from Benita in the schoolyard. He replies 'Good' when she asks how he is and hurries away. It is interpersonal self-protection he is using here. Both are good things, and it is, perhaps, smart for him not to confide in Benita, whom he does not know very well – at any rate, not when he knows that his mother at home is certain to understand him and comfort him and help him get to terms with himself again.

Below are some examples of body language or social actions that are typically used to distance yourself from others.

Body language:

~ avoiding eye contact

~ crossing arms and legs

~ adopting a distant facial expression

~ turning your back or turning to the side.

Social actions:

~ criticising the person who wants to be close to you

~ instigating a conflict,

~ putting others in your debt or simply creating an imbalance by giving a relatively high number of gifts or other favours.

People may use one or more of these or other self-protection strategies without knowing it. In such cases, for example, you may experience dissatisfaction after a conversation without realising that you yourself are preventing the needed closeness.

Some people need to utilise interpersonal self-protection better. I often teach highly sensitive people how they can better shield themselves against other people's confidences when they are overwhelmed or, perhaps, just lack the energy to deal with them.

Highly sensitive people often make far too great a demand on themselves with respect to how attentive they are to the people they are with. For them, it can be a challenge to learn that it is okay to look away or turn aside or even turn their backs when they cannot handle being involved in another person's reality and that it is also okay, for example, to look away when eye contact becomes too overwhelming.

Interpersonal self-protection is an important skill, but it is essential that you know when you make use of it – so you yourself choose when and with whom you want to put a distance, and how great a distance. The same is true of intrapsychic strategies, which I will talk about more in the following section.

Self-protection strategies that distance us from our inner selves

There may be times that are not particularly suited for self-reflection, for example, when you are at work and want to concentrate on that. It may be good to be able to maintain a distance from your inner self, for example, when you are filled with pain, conflict or chaos, or the time and the place are not suited for turning your attention inward.

One of the most fundamental intrapsychic self-protection strategies for achieving this distance is repression, which is a form of forgetting that we choose in the moment or, perhaps, once chose and then forgot the decision to forget. It all just disappeared from our consciousness. We no longer have any idea that one of our parents once abused us in a frightening way.

This can also be expressed in a more physical way: you tense your muscles or stiffen and avoid deep breathing. When we do not want to sense our body, we stop breathing deeply – often, automatically. As a psychotherapist, I pay attention to my client's breathing. I can see how respiration moves to the upper part of the chest when a topic gets too touchy.

Below are several examples of intrapsychic self-protection strategies:

- ~ *Diversion*: For example, we walk around with our iPhone, staying online constantly and checking Facebook at brief intervals.

- ~ *Projection*: We experience the feelings or qualities we have difficulty with as if they belong to other people and not ourselves. For example, when a mother puts a wide-awake child to bed because she feels tired and believes the fatigue belongs to the child.

~ *Making yourself lethargic*: We become lethargic with too much food, entertainment, sleep or other forms of abuse.

~ *We make ourselves blind and deaf to parts of reality*: For example, we do not pay attention to the signs that may exist as to whether other people like us or not. Instead, we build our presumption about this on our own thoughts and fantasies.

~ *Exaggerated positive thinking*: For example, when other people bother us, we always think that, of course, they want the best for us and, in that way, avoid our own anger or grief.

We often have several self-protection strategies going at once, and they can build up layer by layer as in the following example.

Karen's boyfriend looks away every time she asks him whether he is serious about their relationship. If she cannot deal with her own emotional reaction to this, she will protect herself in several ways.

~ She 'avoids' noticing his evasive look (makes herself blind).

~ She sees it and thinks, 'It's just an accident that he happens to look someplace else. Anyway, he told me last year when we were on vacation that he loved me. So, of course, he does' (exaggerated positive thinking).

~ She dares to think the thought: 'Maybe he isn't serious.' At the same time, her breathing moves to the top of her chest (avoidance of deep breathing).

~ She is aware of her superficial breathing and notices that her body has stiffened. She takes a deep breath on purpose and feels the need to check Facebook (diversion).

When we are together with people with whom we feel safe, we can give expression to more of ourselves. In the best case scenario, Karen will dare to think the thought all the way through and feel her own emotional reaction when she is together with a close friend who is good at listening and supporting her.

In the worst case, she has so many self-protection strategies going that she has no friends in which she can confide. In that case, she risks continuing to protect herself and may stay with him several more years without ever testing properly how serious he really is.

The balance between intrapsychic and interpersonal self-protection

Interpersonal self-protection strategies keep other people from getting too close, and intrapsychic self-protection strategies protect you from your own thoughts, feelings and desires. But your own internal emotional state and the closeness or absence of other people are closely connected. As human beings, we arouse many different feelings and reactions in each other – and intrapsychic and interpersonal self-protection strategies can supplement each other.

People who have strong self-protection strategies against their inner selves do not need much protection externally. They will typically seem robust and able to handle a great deal of social contact.

These people will typically be very open and communicative, will not experience much anxiety, and will seem to be in touch with their emotions and know themselves. But, possibly, the 'self' they know and identify with is a self they have partially invented themselves. And, possibly, the feelings they talk about are pseudo-feelings – feelings they have imagined or decided to have rather than emotions they actually feel. They have a social mask with which they identify completely while they have no contact with their deeper feelings and desires. A statement such as 'I am always happy' indicates that the person is not in touch with his or her true feelings.

The weaker your intrapsychic self-protection strategies are, the more interpersonal self-protection strategies you need. People whose self-protection strategies against their inner selves are weak need strong external strategies to protect them from the outside world. They easily become overwhelmed by social contact and need to withdraw to find themselves.

The self-protection strategies of highly sensitive people against their inner selves are typically thinner than most. They have easier access to their unconscious and feel their inner selves more strongly than most other people do.

Therefore, some very sensitive people choose to keep away from other people for periods of time. Isolating yourself is the safest way to avoid closeness either because it is too overwhelming or because it awakens old wounds of the heart.

The same person can have both too little and too much self-protection. It is not always an either–or. For many people, it may be advantageous to get rid of obsolete or superficial self-protection strategies in some areas while, in other areas, it might be better to fortify themselves by building up new ones.

It is a strength if we ourselves choose to employ a self-protection technique or not. But it can lead to problems if we employ it without being aware of it – and we have a hard time understanding why something else happens in our contact with other people than what we intended consciously. I shall talk about how this can happen in the next chapter.

Chapter 2

WHEN SELF-PROTECTION STRATEGIES BECOME AUTOMATIC

Let us return to the story about Jasper, who hurt his knee on the way to school and used different self-protection strategies to keep himself from feeling something. Let us say that another boy, Martin, had the same experience but came home to a mother who was unable to provide the right kind of help. Maybe she told him that it was nothing to cry about or that he should just fight back. Martin would then have returned to school the next day unresolved. He would have needed to use energy to suppress his fear of the big boys and keep the lump in his throat under control.

In the best case scenario, he would go to some other adult, for example, Benita from the schoolyard. But there is a chance that he would not seek out any other adult out of loyalty to his mother or because he has become afraid of his own feelings, which his mother has failed to validate.

If he decides to distance himself from his inner feelings (just as his mother has done) and needs contact with an adult at school, it will not be Benita, who would respond to him with empathy. This is because empathy would threaten the armour he has built up around himself.

If another person sees feelings we do not want to be in contact with at the moment, it amplifies them and makes it impossible to hold them back.

If Martin wants to distance himself from his feelings, he has to protect himself from the kindness of others because any concerned attention may threaten his self-control. So, if he needs an adult, he will choose Mr Riber instead of Benita. Mr Riber is a cold person who is distracted and has no antennae out for Martin's vulnerability.

If this behaviour, which is interpersonal self-protection, is repeated so often that it finally becomes automatic and unconscious, Martin as an adult will no longer realise, for example, that he consistently chooses partners who are cold or, to some degree, emotionally inaccessible.

When self-protection strategies have become automatic and unconscious, we can get very lost. We cannot understand why we always run into obstacles or continue to repeat reactions or patterns that we do not want but cannot get rid of.

A self-protection strategy does not need to be used very many times in childhood before it becomes automatic. It is, in a way, like learning to ride a bicycle. At the beginning, we think a lot about how we put our feet on the pedals and in what order. We go to a lot of trouble to put our hands correctly on the handlebars to keep our balance. But once we have learned to ride a bike, we do it from then on without thinking about what we are really doing. In the same way, we can live with a self-protection technique that we no longer realise is there or even that we ourselves have initiated it.

Self-protection strategies are most often unconscious; and, sometimes, we live with them for so long that we think they are a part of our personality.

How you can merge with your own self-protection strategies will be elaborated in the next section.

When self-protection strategies become part of our self-understanding

It can be difficult to distinguish self-protection strategies from our own personality.

People who think of their self-protection strategies as a part of themselves will, of course, react angrily if others point them out and suggest alternative ways to make contact with other people. Perhaps they say, 'Don't try to change me. I'm the kind of person who does not need other people to take care of me. I am a person who likes to take care of myself. You have to learn to accept that this is how I work.' And if someone questions this, they will take it as a personal attack.

If you have completely identified with your self-protection strategies, the first step is to realise that there are components in the way you work that distance you from other people, from being able to sense your inner feelings clearly and, perhaps, from being able to see your own life situation clearly. The next step is to find the desire and courage to change this.

If you are aware that you sometimes trip yourself up and destroy your chances to form closer relationships with other people and yourself, you are well on the way. It is not certain you have a very precise understanding of what it is you do to avoid the closeness you long for. But if you are open and interested in finding out, you are already on the way.

Why such powerful self-protection strategies exist – particularly when it comes to love relationships – is what the next chapter is about.

Chapter 3

FEAR OF CLOSENESS, GRIEF AND LOSS OF CONTROL

Beyond the accompanying joy and increase in quality of life, entering into a loving relationship can lead to sorrow in two ways. One is the sorrow of losing all your other opportunities. When we decide to bond with a particular partner, we reject many other possible partners. No one has everything we want. So, when we choose a particular person, we must let go of the notion of getting from a partner things the chosen one does not have. This is one sorrow. The other sorrow lies ahead, because a loving relationship is a sorrow that has not yet occurred. We lose those we love – if not before, then when one of us dies. If you are very afraid of loss and sorrow, you may have an unconscious resistance to letting other people have meaning in your life.

If you are good at grieving, the idea of another loss is not nearly as frightening. If you know about yourself that you can live through a sorrow and find your way to the other side with renewed love of life and new insight, you are not going to be afraid to the same degree.

Being able to mourn and give time to it is extremely important but not something that is given much attention in our time. Every so often, I hear clients say that they had not been down in the dumps for very long before they were offered antidepressants and felt pressured to get quickly back up to speed and deal with the challenges of the workplace. This is unfortunate, because the ability to love and the ability to grieve are inextricably linked.

Ursula, who had several relationships behind her and was on her way into a new one, was completely aware of the risk that this new relationship would only be of a short duration. But she did not hold herself back. As she said, 'I've experienced loss before and know it is not dangerous. Some days, I cry and find someone to talk to about it. And, then, it's a question of time before I'm ready to take a new chance.' If you are afraid of grief and loss, loving relationships are highly risky affairs.

If you have experienced loss earlier in life that you have tried to avoid feeling and, therefore, have not processed properly, it can be said that you are carrying around avoided grief. If you do that, the fear of new loss will be increased.

As a psychotherapist, I find that a surprising number of people have major or minor avoided griefs as part of their baggage. It may be some young love or a childhood grief such as, for example, a beloved grandparent or some other person who died when they were too small to understand what 'never again' means. In many cases, they did not get any help for it because, until a few decades ago, people wanted to 'spare' children from knowing about death by not talking to them about it and, typically, not taking them to the funeral.

Many people 'forget' an important person who suddenly disappeared because the loss is connected with so much sorrow and confusion that it is nicer not to remember. But if you lug around avoided grief, you will be especially afraid of new sorrows. We know intuitively that new sorrows stir up old ones and risk destroying the self-protection there is in having forgotten both the distress and the person who was dear to us.

Avoided grief often shows up in psychotherapy, and there may be great liberation in re-remembering someone dear to us and re-integrating that person's resources and the nice feelings connected with him or her into your own personality. But many people remain unconscious of this sort of grief for their entire lives and have developed a number of inappropriate self-protection strategies that prevent sorrow from being acknowledged.

One way of avoiding old and new sorrows is to avoid forming deep attachments. Some people have no loving relationships – only relationships of the type we might call exchange relationships. We exchange services. You listen to my frustrations, and I listen to yours. We divert and entertain each other. There is nothing wrong with exchange relationships, but you miss out on something if that is the only type of relationship you have. On the other hand, you are not particularly exposed to sorrow. An exchange relationship can be replaced relatively easily. It is far more difficult to find a replacement if you have gone so deeply into a relationship that the other person has become utterly unique for you, and your happiness has to some degree become connected with – and, perhaps, dependent on – him or her.

Many marriages are, in reality, exchange relationships. The couple meet each other's needs or some of them and get cheaper living expenses since there are two of them. But they cannot – or can no longer – light up each other's eyes or make each other's inner gardens blossom.

If you avoid entering into loving relationships, you secure yourself against great loss.

Many people do not even realise that they have an inner conflict. They are themselves of the conviction that they really want to enter into a loving relationship – and wonder why something always gets in the way. But, unconsciously, they work from a completely different interest: an interest in protecting themselves from pain. And, therefore, they have developed different strategies to keep a relationship from having so much meaning that its loss will be too painful or too overwhelming the day the relationship is over.

Or they cannot handle the grief of missed opportunities and, therefore, dare not choose anything.

This is not about the fact that some people have courage while others are cowards in this area. The reason people lack courage, as a rule, is that they have experienced great pain early in life and have received no help. Therefore, they are extremely sensitive to the loss of love.

One client relates:

Once, I just didn't want to have anything to do with the rules of life's game. I wanted both love *and* security. Now, I have realised that I can choose between wasting my life hunting for security, which has far too high a price, or I can start getting used to swimming in life's currents. With great fear and trembling, I'm trying to do the latter.

Some people avoid entering into loving relationships by utilising self-protection strategies, which I will describe in the following chapter.

Chapter 4

UNFORTUNATE PATTERNS THAT CAN HINDER A SUCCESSFUL LOVE LIFE

In this chapter, I shall describe different patterns and strategies that are typical for people who have problems with their love life.

Going for the two birds in the bush

A bird in the hand is worth two in the bush – so goes the old saying. One way of avoiding closeness is to focus your attention consistently and exclusively on the birds in the bush outside your reach.

One example is Sophia, who had many fantasies of connecting with people who were unreachable. It might, for example, be a person who is in another relationship. Or someone who is so beautiful, clever or rich that the chances he or she would choose her were small.

Another example is Ida. She consistently fell for people who were not interested in her. She herself thought no one wanted her while, in reality, it was the case that she had unconsciously sensed from far away a man's degree of interest in her. If it was small, her own interest combusted, and all her fantasies took flight. She felt a flowering of positive feelings inside and imagined how much she would be able to love this particular man. But the fact of the matter was that she was once so hurt that she would never dare to love or be dependent on other people. As long as the desired person was unachievable, she could have her fantasies in peace.

When Ida met a man who showed her his undivided positive interest, she became afraid, and another self-protection strategy was employed. Let us call this one 'find five mistakes'. She would notice that the man's trousers were a little too short and found this humiliating. Or she focused on the thickness of his thighs and thought, 'Such thick thighs. I could never be turned on by that.' It might also be other details that suddenly had great significance and became a huge problem. So, she dumped him right away.

Ida often said that she would like to have a partner but was unaware herself of how afraid she actually was. Beginning a relationship with a specific, reachable man would also be rejecting all the other possible men she was dreaming about. Moreover, a concrete man has his limitations, and he has his own needs and wants to exist for his own sake. As long as you are dreaming of wonderful, unreachable men, it is possible to imagine the impossible: unconditional love in unlimited quantities.

Dorothy had a similar pattern. She had been married to Bert for many years but never managed to achieve the closeness she needed. When she started therapy, she was fixated on everything that was wrong with him. But, later, she discovered that she was using the 'find five mistakes' strategy every time he offered her closeness and intimacy – and that, in those situations, she very easily started a fight.

It turned out that Dorothy was afraid of being emotionally dependent on her husband. She had found security in taking care of herself on an emotional level.

Then, she did not need to be so afraid of losing him and, thus, so afraid of not being able to maintain her own limits in relation to him. The day Sophia, Ida and Dorothy dared to feel and admit how afraid they actually were, personal growth could begin, and they were gradually able to dismantle some of the strategies that were preventing them from finding what they were looking for.

To secure yourself from heartache by relegating most of your love life in the imagination alone and avoiding close relationships in one way or another is one of the many ways we can protect ourselves. Below, I shall indicate some of the other traps you can fall into when you are trying to protect yourself.

If you kiss a frog, he becomes a prince

Some people consistently choose to court a potential partner who does not have much to give or may have neither the desire nor the talent for much closeness and warmth. What turns them on may be the dream that this closed person must have an enormous need for love and tenderness deep inside and how happy he will be for it.

The concept of saving someone else may provide a false sense of security because you believe that a partner you have saved from the darkness must be so grateful, happy and dependent on his saviour that you can be sure of never being abandoned.

But what typically happens is that he does not change even though she kisses him and kisses him for many years. Or that he actually does change and, with his new self-confidence, goes out into the world and finds another. For how can you stand being with someone to whom you owe so much?

In this trap, you try to procure both love *and* security. And, as it goes so often, someone who wants everything ultimately ends up with nothing.

Waiting for the perfect person

It actually happens that people who have not been in any relationship for many years one day meet someone with whom they can bond.

But insisting on finding someone who is 100 per cent right is most often a utopia and a self-protection strategy. If you can be satisfied with a partner who is 51 per cent right, the chances of being satisfied in a couple relationship are far greater. Moreover, it may turn out that, if we give ourselves to a person who is 51 per cent right, the person's percentage of 'rightness' will grow, and we ourselves will be changed in the encounter, so something entirely new suddenly becomes possible. The person who, at the start, might just be better than nothing may end up being the 'right one' if both partners dare to go deeply enough into the relationship and give it a chance.

Another way of trying to achieve security is to struggle to become the 'right one' yourself. More on that in the next section.

The struggle to be the 'right one'

Many people struggle their whole lives to become good enough. 'Good enough' for most people means so good that they can be sure other people will not reject them. To be sure of being loved tomorrow and forever. It is a project that is doomed to failure from the start. For someone to try to be good enough to be certain in their relationships is an illusion. It is a security that does not exist.

No one can be sure that those whom they love will not change tastes or take a different direction in life. Because life is a movement. We are always in the process of changing, and the art is to dare to be present in the now and go with the flow.

If you insist on playing the role of the 'right one', genuine presence will be difficult to achieve, because good, life-giving contact with another person demands that both dare to stand by themselves for good or bad.

As we have seen, a person may be employing many different unconscious strategies to avoid sorrow and pain. These same strategies, unfortunately, often have the effect of avoiding what you long for most deeply. Below, we shall look at one self-protection strategy that often lays the groundwork for many of the others.

Many people have created an internal picture of their parents and their childhood that is gilded in relation to reality. If you see your parents as ideal figures and not as the ordinary people they were or are, you distance yourself from reality, and that can make it harder to navigate in life.

Chapter 5

Parental Idealisation

Some people have a very gilded recollection of their childhood and their parents. When Iris came to therapy for the first time, she was convinced that there had been no problems in her childhood home:

> I can't understand why my life has been so hard because I had a fantastic childhood. My parents loved me very much. My mother was a housewife. There was always somebody at home. It was really secure. I had an extremely secure childhood. I think it's embarrassing that I'm sitting here now with you. Nobody knows – and my parents especially must never find out.

No one has had a childhood that was exclusively good. There are no perfect parents, and we have all been damaged to greater or lesser degrees. Some people think that their childhood was only good.

In my experience, there is a correlation between how many positive superlatives a person uses when she describes her childhood and her parents and how distressing her childhood must actually have been. In Iris's case, it proved later in the course of therapy that her childhood was actually impoverished of love and genuine interest.

People who have had a predominantly good childhood do not need to emphasise how good it all was. They speak about their parents with warmth and gratitude. They can speak easily about what was good and what was difficult.

The clients who insist they had an exclusively good childhood often use the following argument for the indisputable excellence of their father and mother: 'They have always been very interested in me.' This gives rise to a talk about what 'interest' really means in the relationship between parents and children.

Two forms of interest can be distinguished. You can have an interest in whether someone is doing well. I can have an interest in whether my partner, for example, is doing well because it affects my mood, my finances and my social status. And all parents have an interest in whether their children are doing well. Then, they can feel like they are good parents; they feel joy in their children's happiness and pride in their offspring. You can have an interest in other people in the same way that you can have an interest in acquiring things you are going to use for something or other.

Having a caring interest *for* your child's (or your partner's) inner feelings is something else. To be interested in understanding another person as well as possible, to want to go exploring and discover the unique personality the other person has, to be interested in the other's inner life for their own sake and on that person's terms, is something completely different from having an interest *in* it.

At one point far into therapy, a client told me:

> I can see now that I grew up as a thing. No one was interested in learning to know my inner self. No one asked what I wanted deep inside, what I hoped for. My parents acted as if they knew in advance – without having investigated it – who I was. And I tried to be the person they had decided in advance to see me as.

Gradually, she was able to remember and feel the loneliness of her childhood and appreciate herself for the great work she was engaged in: first, by stopping the attempt to be the person her parents saw, and then by finding out who she really was.

interest in | interest for

During the course of therapy, one woman became painfully conscious of how much she herself as a mother had an interest in rather than for. As she put it:

> When I became a mother, I was terribly afraid I wasn't good enough. When I looked at my son, I was obsessed with seeing signs of whether I was good enough or not. If he was sad, I saw it as a sign that I was no good and couldn't stand to be with him in his sadness but found, instead, a thousand activities to make him happy. There was not much left over for me to have an interest for his inner self – for his own sake.

When I speak to clients about their childhood, they often become very obsessed with their own parenting skills and very sad at discovering their own shortcomings. This is often a form of self-protection, a defence against looking at their parents' faults – after all, it is better to be obsessed with their own faults (an obsession that has followed them all of their lives). In this way, they protect their inner image of Mum and Dad for a while longer because, even though they have discovered that Mum and Dad were not as perfect as they first believed, the faults of Mum and Dad were petty in comparison to the client's own!

This does not mean that it might not be a good idea to take up their own parental role for review and, perhaps, use their new recognitions to improve relations with their own children. Here, it is important to remember, before one gets too lost in guilt feelings, that no parent is perfect and no children avoid scrapes and bruises. And that's good. Scrapes and bruises often provide nice opportunities for growth. And a certain amount of adversity is good for children and young people. It helps mature them, so they develop sides of themselves that otherwise might have remained in hibernation.

It is actually a heroic feat to give our children just a little more than we got ourselves – because it is especially difficult to provide something you have not gotten yourself. If we succeed, we nudge our legacy in a positive direction. To believe that you can do everything right as a parent is a path to defeat and crisis the day reality shows its face.

When I question a client's image of his or her parents, the client often becomes very frantic and irritable. Just speaking about it can feel very unpleasant. 'I feel so disloyal' is one line I often hear in this context. We are in a dangerous area. Parental idealisation is often one of the main pillars in the structure of a person's self-protection strategies.

Why not leave their parental idealisation in peace? Because parental idealisation has a high price. If you cannot see your parents as they are or were in reality, you cannot see yourself.

An idealised parental image may affect your image of yourself in two ways. More on this in the following two sections.

Parental idealisation and self-idealisation

Our experience of our parents as fantastic may be linked to a conception of ourselves being the same. A person with this self-perception may have a tendency to believe that the difficulties he has in life are due to other people or external circumstances. Maybe he views others as being envious of him. It may also be, he thinks, that he has been unfortunate in his choice of partners or that he has a horrible boss who does not see him as he really is.

He may even find that, if his wife did not have so many problems or if his employer were not so unsympathetic or whatever he might think is wrong with his external circumstances, he would be happy and live a good life.

His most important self-protection strategy is projection. Instead of acknowledging his own problematic sides, he sees everything that is negative in other people.

I rarely encounter clients with this sort of distortion in their understanding – of their parents and themselves – in psychotherapy. They simply do not see themselves as needing therapy. However, I often see those close to them – their wives, husbands or children. They are having a hard time and often suffer from low self-esteem. Often, without knowing it themselves, they are carrying around the dark sides of the self-idealising person, which the self-idealising person does not dare feel or acknowledge.

Parental idealisation and self-devaluation

Parental idealisation may also be linked to self-devaluation. If there is nothing wrong with Mum and Dad, why do I have problems? The answer seems to be 'Because I'm not good enough!' Here, you make your parents better than they are and yourself worse.

Some people pay the price for maintaining their image of Mum and Dad as good parents with low self-esteem and bad thoughts about themselves. It could be said that the 'I'm not good enough' attitude protects parental idealisation, which in turn protects the person from experiencing the feeling of not being loved enough or, even worse, not being loved at all. And it was a good strategy once.

As adults, however, most of us can tolerate the feeling of not being loved. When we dare to feel this emotion as a part of our inner experience, we cast off many of the self-protection 'scams' that take us away from life and ourselves.

Some people alternate between these two pits. During some periods, they see themselves as fantastic while, at other times, they see themselves as worthless.

These two traps correspond to the fact that you can repeat patterns from childhood in two ways. There is an active form in which you identify with your parents and treat others the way your parents treated you. If, for example, your parents criticised you time and again, you will as an adult criticise others.

You can also repeat patterns from childhood in a more passive form. In this case, you find yourself with people who criticise you and subject you to criticism without any serious resistance because it feels familiar and natural to be in that role.

If you repeat your parents' patterns in a passive or active form, you are – as long as you are not conscious of what is going on – complicit in accepting the pattern and protecting your parents' behaviour against question and criticism.

I shall talk more about how parental idealisation might once have been a good solution to a difficult situation in the next section.

When we alter reality

Many children who grow up with parents who lack something fundamental on the emotional level will do what they can to avoid examining their parents' flaws. There are two reasons for this. One is that small children see themselves as a part of their parents and, for that reason, necessarily experience them as good. The other reason is that the very notion that the two adults who have responsibility for a child's welfare and survival might lack parental competence is so frightening to little children that it is quickly repressed. They will, instead, create an inner image of Mum and Dad as strong, competent and loving – even though this is not the case in reality. At the same time, children make themselves blind and deaf to signs of the opposite.

This sort of strategy is expedient for small children, who are too fragile to deal with such a frightening reality. Children compensate for these deficiencies and create another reality in their imagination in which they can find the necessary security.

The problem arises when, as an adult, you continue to trust your conceptions more than the reality in your life. If you have idealised father and mother and made yourself deaf and blind to their less advantageous sides, you will probably do the same in your relationships with your children or partners. And you remain defenceless and alone.

One woman who, throughout her life, had trusted her own fantasies more than what she sensed in the moment exclaimed at the end of a long process of therapy:

> I'm shaken when I look back now and see that I have actually had a long-lasting relationship with a man without at any point examining properly whether he even liked me. I just

told myself, 'Of course he does.' But now when I see reality in a clearer light, I can see that this was not the case.

This is an example of how badly things can go if you are guided to a greater degree by your own thinking or imagination than what you sense in the actual life situation.

In the next section, there will be an example of how a self-protection strategy can arise and how it can wreak havoc on your love life.

Forgotten decisions

You may have taken many decisions early in your life that you no longer remember. One middle-aged man relates:

> I decided once when I was very small that I would take care of myself and would not be dependent on any other people. When I took that decision, it was the only option I could see at that moment.

It does not take much time for such decisions to become unconscious, and those parts of the personality that are in conflict with the decision are erased from consciousness. Not long afterwards, he no longer knew that he had a yearning for love and a desire to be closely connected to other people.

Most self-protection strategies arise early in childhood. They were once the best solution the little child could find to a difficult situation. Later, self-protection strategies become unconscious and engage automatically every time we enter into a situation that resembles one of the unresolved crises of our childhood.

Here is one example.

Maria wondered why she sometimes snapped at her boyfriend when he approached her in a loving way. The answer must be found in the situation in which the self-protection strategy arose. The situation must be relived, processed and retold in a new way.

Maria had a narrative that went like this: 'Deep down, I'm not worth loving; but, if I keep others at a distance, they don't find that out.'

She herself does not realise that she once took the decision to keep others at a distance. But it quickly turned up when she began to direct her attention toward the strategies she utilises today. After working through the situations in which Maria's narrative about herself arose, a far more realistic tale comes out. Maria's new narrative goes like this:

> I was once a child in need, and my parents lacked the necessary skills to help me. I was not the one with the problem. I was a completely ordinary child who was having a hard time and tried to solve some problems that no child – no matter how clever – could solve alone.
>
> Now I'm grown and no longer dependent on other people to the same life-and-death degree. Life is not so dangerous any more, and it's okay to experiment with closeness to others and see whether it might be comfortable for me to give a little more of myself.

Maria's new narrative gave her more self-esteem and the courage to take a new decision – that, from now on, she would practise letting those close to her come closer.

Below is another example of a self-protection strategy that can have fatal consequences if it is not revised during one's adult life.

When we are against ourselves

Children who are unsure whether they are loved will be inclined to take the side of their parents against themselves. When children like this are scolded, you can afterwards hear them walking around and scolding themselves with the same words mother or father used. When children do this, they identify with Mum and Dad, and it gives them the sense of being with them.

When you are against yourself, you are very alone – but, for a small child, it is better to abandon yourself than lose a vital and necessary connection to your father or mother.

The problem arises if, when significant people in our lives direct their anger against us, we as adults immediately take their side – against ourselves. Then, we become defenceless and very alone. Who will be with us?

It is not certain that we ourselves realise that we too easily take the side of others against ourselves. We may only experience it as feeling bad when a significant person in our lives is dissatisfied with us.

I was amazed to discover how many of the people I meet in psychotherapy go around scolding themselves or just speaking badly to themselves – without being aware of it. There is one question I ask again and again: 'What did you say to yourself at that moment?' And the client's answer sometimes reveals a condescending or just very unkind remark that he or she is shaken to discover.

Of course, it is good to keep a critical eye on yourself and, sometimes, concede others are right when they are dissatisfied with something you have said or done. It is only wrong if self-criticism or self-recrimination becomes an un-nuanced and automatic form of behaviour that makes you feel bad without being able to control it.

Taking the side of others against yourself is a self-protection strategy called 'identification with the aggressor'. In the same way as parental idealisation, it can protect against the feeling of loneliness and the sense of not being loved. But, as an adult, it can create problems in your love life.

For Jared, whom we shall meet in the following example, the problem was that, again and again, he entered into relationships with women who did not appreciate him. The woman in his last relationship, for example, asked him to do various practical chores for her as if this were completely self-evident. She did not even ask in a polite way or make coffee for him when he came over. He watched enviously how his friends found women who were loving and went out of their way with their appearance and what they served. Jared continued to enter into one unsatisfactory relationship after another until he worked through a trauma from his childhood. Jared relates:

> I remember that I was beaten as a child but not what it felt like. I just have a vague recollection that I tried to make myself emotionless.
>
> When I started talking about it in psychotherapy, greater and greater nuance began appearing in my recollections, and my feelings from that time began slowly over many weeks to grow closer and closer. I began to feel what it was like to be a child who was beaten by someone they loved and trusted.
>
> It was like being in the middle of a nightmare in which the sun was about to disappear from the sky while the moon was crashing into the earth at a furious speed. Totally without mitigating circumstances. In the nightmare, I discovered that there was a part of me that took my father's side and thought I deserved to be treated so badly. When I relinquished this alliance (identification with the aggressor),

I could accept myself as the child I was then. Among other things, a child who wanted life so much that he went along with being wrong in order to preserve the necessary feeling of connectedness with his father.

Afterwards, I could say to myself what an adult should have said to me then – namely, that it was not me there was something wrong with. What was going on around me was wrong, and that was the responsibility of the adults – not me.

I promised myself never again to go along with being poorly treated.

In one period, I stood up for myself if anyone spoke to me in an unfriendly tone. Now I have found some balance in which I can accept that others may be having a bad day without the energy left for kindness – without it being their intention to take it out on me. But I have become much better at respecting myself, and I will no longer enter into relationships in which I do not feel validated.

People who have experienced being 'beaten' with words will probably also recognise themselves in Jared's account. Being beaten by someone you love when you are a child is destructive of your own worth. If you have 'forgotten' the event in order to protect your inner image of a good parent, you do not look for the necessary help and risk letting yourself be beaten throughout your life without properly defending yourself because, somewhere deep inside you, you are hiding experiences that have unconsciously spawned a belief that you do not deserve better.

If, in your childhood, you have been treated as a 'thing' whose inner life no one is interested in listening to or creating contact with, you may easily allow this to happen in the present. In that case, you repeat the pattern from childhood in a passive form in which you play the same role in adult life you did when you were a child.

The reverse can also be the case – namely, that you treat others as things in the same way your parents did. This is the active form for the repetition of childhood patterns. In this way, what you yourself have suffered is taken out on other people. It may, for example, be your partner, who may be a tool for you – more than a person you are trying to connect with. He or she may, for example, be a means for avoiding pain from your childhood. And the expectations for your partner or what you want out of a relationship in general may be out of proportion. I shall talk more about that in the next section.

Unconscious expectations for a partner to compensate for deficiencies in childhood

If you have not grieved yourself free or let go of what you did not get from Mum and Dad in childhood, you will typically insist on getting it from your partner. Probably, you yourself do not realise the mechanism but simply feel deep frustration at your partner.

The less conscious you are about the mechanism, the greater the risk that you will begin to nag your partner and completely overlook that person's right to be themselves on their own premises.

In short, the mechanism is that you insist on having had a better childhood than is the case – your partner must compensate for what was lacking and, in that way, make sure you do not feel the void. If your partner does not succeed in doing that, he will be on the receiving end of all the anger and dissatisfaction, and you will behave like a demanding infant.

Hannah relates:

When I started therapy, I had had a series of relationships that lasted less than a year. I was good at taking the initiative and meeting men. The 'falling in love' stage was, as a rule, pretty much problem free. When it began to become 'everyday', I typically felt a form of emptiness inside that I could not stand. It might be, for example, if my boyfriend decided to do something with others, and I was alone and felt rejected. I would go to pieces – tears and rage. I could hardly contain myself. 'It can't be true that you feel so bad when you have a boyfriend,' I thought. I wanted to make my partner feel guilty and was really mean. I might call him ten times in an evening or keep him awake all night with all my frustration and anger. I just didn't have it in me to try to see the situation from his side.

When I look back now on my behaviour, I'm amazed any of the men stuck around as long as they did.

When Hannah gave up her parental idealisation and the huge demands she made upon her partner, it was connected to great grief – both grief over the loveless life she was living now and over her emotionally impoverished childhood.

But grief was not as heavy to bear as the sadness she had lived with for long periods of her life. In the midst of her grief, she felt more alive than she had done in a long time, and she felt more authentically present in her relationships. She found that the road from tears to laughter can be quite short and felt how life giving it was to share these emotions with the people who were in her life.

In our culture, we typically expect that grief is heavy, dark and long lasting. In reality, grief is sometimes only warm, wet and heartening.

The reward of seeing parents
in a more realistic light

Re-examining your relationship with or view of your father, your mother or your own childhood is something many people resist. It may be unpleasant to look hard at your own past if it has not been optimal.

However, it can be rewarding to overcome your reluctance because the closer we get to a realistic view of our parents and ourselves, the better we can commit ourselves to close relationships – and deal with life in general. The more we are in harmony with ourselves and find repose in knowing who we are, the greater the chances are that we will find something that will give our lives meaning and fullness.

The strategies we use with other people have arisen in relation to our closest caregivers when we were children. The less our parents have been able to deal with us and teach us healthy relationship skills, the more self-protection strategies we will have going as adults.

On the other hand, when we let go of a self-protection strategy, it will be experienced as a liberation and provide renewed hope and lust for life as it did for Jared in the example below. He was over 50 before he began to work on his relationship with his problematic father. Jared tells about a breakthrough that took place at the end of a long process of therapy:

> Even though my father punished us children harshly, I had always been convinced that, deep inside, he loved me. I remember my therapist questioned this conviction, and now she sat there, giving me this sad and deeply serious look while I propounded one argument after another to prove that my conviction was correct.

At one point, she said, 'You seem very frantic. I wonder what that's about?' I felt completely empty inside. Then, my body began to tremble and the tears flowed. It was as if my body understood before my head did. Then, I felt liberated. It was as if, in that moment, I found a piece of myself.

It can be very liberating to look directly at reality even though we often try to defend ourselves against it if it is frightening or just uncomfortable.

If it is not worked through, parental idealisation may create problems in close relationships

Our parents taught us love and connection as well as they could. If we have not consciously taken a position on the way we relate to others, we will most likely behave the way Mum and Dad did and speak to ourselves the way they spoke to us. And we will act in roughly the same way on the emotional level as they did – since they were the ones who taught us this.

We will probably, then, find a partner who has roughly the same attitude toward love and connection. At any rate, it will feel familiar and safe, and it will be easy for us to deal with.

It can also be a self-protection strategy to avoid beginning a relationship with someone who can do more on the emotional plane than Mum and Dad. If we find a partner who can do more than our progenitors, we have to learn something new. And we also have to see our parents in a new light: namely, as people who could not and, therefore, have not taught us something important about love and relationships.

An idealisation of parents who have deficient parenting skills may give little children a feeling of security, which is extremely necessary for their psychic health. However, the same idealisation can give adults problems in their love life.

Working toward a more nuanced and precise understanding of who these two people were or are is a lifelong task that we never finish just as we never finish discovering and understanding ourselves.

Understanding comes in layers. We may think we know the full truth until the day we suddenly understand our lives at a deeper level; and then, in hindsight, we can see that what we first believed we had understood completely was just the top of the iceberg.

The deeper the understanding, the greater the liberation. So, even though we have worked with a problem or a dilemma before, it can often be very worthwhile to look at it again. And this is especially true with respect to such an important part of our lives as our relationship with our parents.

If we want to improve our relationship skills, however, the first step is to examine the strategies we are using here and now.

It is not always necessary to go back and work on your relationship with your closest caregivers in childhood. In some cases, you can settle for changing a few habits in the present and laying the foundation for changing unfortunate patterns – whether they are in thought or in action.

But if this present-oriented approach does not work, there is the option of going to the root of the patterns. It may be a hard, bloody road; but, in my experience, if you carefully dig down to the bottom of the situations in which the strategies arose, there is a good chance of achieving fundamental changes in both behaviour and mood.

In the next chapter, we shall look at how it feels when there are no self-protection strategies to prevent us from getting in touch with ourselves.

Chapter 6

TOTAL CONSCIOUSNESS
OF AN EMOTION

Knowing precisely what you feel is a big help for navigating in your life – particularly in human relationships. But what would it mean to be totally conscious of your feelings in the now?

If you are totally conscious of an emotion, you can experience it in three ways:[1]

~ in your body

~ as an impulse (desire)

~ with your understanding.

Here is an example using the feeling of anxiety:

~ In our bodies, for example, we feel ourselves trembling.

~ The impulse may be a desire to run away screaming.

~ With our understanding, we know we are afraid.

Let's take another example, the feeling of anger:

~ In our bodies, we feel warmth and, perhaps, a quivering sensation.

---

1   If we cannot feel an emotion in all three ways, however, this need not be due to self-protection strategies. There may also be other reasons – for example, that you have not learned it.

~ The impulse, for example, may be a desire to strike out.

~ With our understanding, we know that we are angry.

And from joy:

~ In our bodies, we feel a sparkling sensation inside.

~ The impulse may be a desire to break out into spontaneous song.

~ With our understanding, we know we are happy.

Out of self-protection, you may have repressed one mode of experience. Some people do not pay attention to their bodies at all but experience themselves primarily from the neck up. Others have difficulty understanding their own feelings. And others, in turn, cannot sense what they desire. In psychotherapy, I find that it is most often the impulse, the emotion's inherent desire, which is unconscious.

A great deal of shame can be found here. If, for example, you want to sit on your boss's lap and ask for some attention or to make erotic approaches to someone who is 30 years younger or in a relationship with someone else, you may experience embarrassment or shame.

It is often tempting to repress or to deny such a desire.

Some people are afraid that they won't be able to keep themselves from doing it if they allow themselves to experience the desire in its full strength. But feeling your desire and making room for the fantasy connected to it is not dangerous. The better you can deal with your desires and wants, the less risk there is you will lose control and do something you will find wrong or embarrassing.

The desire that is in anger, of course, may be a frightening thing to feel – especially if the anger is powerful. If you have a desire to destroy something for somebody or hurt another person, you may have some powerful guilt feelings. However, there is no ground for this because you are not master over your desires. You cannot decide it will go away. At most, you can repress it, and this does not make it less dangerous – to the contrary. You cannot be guilty about something you have no influence over. My book *Highly Sensitive People in an Insensitive World* (Sand 2016a) goes into more depth about how influence is a prerequisite for guilt.

As far as feelings are concerned, you are better off letting them be as they are and invite them into your total consciousness in all three modes of experience. Then, you'll find that they are not dangerous in themselves. We determine for ourselves whether we act upon a desire in our lives – and we can choose not to if our conscience forbids it or if we find it too embarrassing.

Useful information can be found in these impulses. If you have a desire to hit another person, it is often because you feel you have been 'hit' by him or her. You can use this knowledge to gain greater insight into yourself.

If you can sense your emotion in all three modes, you are totally conscious of the emotion and are close to your own inner reality. But it is possible that the emotion you are sensing is secondary, covering up another feeling that reflects even better what you are feeling at the moment – and which could bring you even closer to yourself if you were to examine it.

One example might be anger, which covers up fear. A father who scolds his teenage daughter for coming home later than they had agreed is probably more afraid than angry even though it is the anger that he immediately feels and expresses. If he allows himself to feel how afraid he has been, lying awake at night waiting for her, he gets closer to himself. And closer to his daughter if he dares to tell her that.

Many of us find it is easier to make room for anger than, for example, fear and uncertainty. More on that in the next section.

Feelings may be found in layers, one on top of the other

It is a feature of anger to be on top, to cover up other feelings. This is especially true for men. Depressed men feel and often express anger even when their primary feeling is sadness or powerlessness. Anger is a powerful emotion – in anger, we fight. The problem is if what we are fighting for with anger is impossible. Or if anger keeps at a distance the people whose concern we actually need most – perhaps without knowing it. The angry man who dares to feel and express how powerless and sad he feels attracts concern and is closer to feeling better about himself than the one who remains trapped in anger.

Anxiety may also be a top-layer emotion, covering up a forbidden joy, a powerful anger or, perhaps, just a conflict with your own self-image. Anxiety may also be expressed in a manner that resembles sorrow because it is accompanied by tears.

Even though you are totally conscious of a feeling, you can sometimes get even closer to your authentic inner self by asking yourself whether this feeling might be covering up something that is even more crucial to you right now. You can learn more about how to become more precise in sensing and knowing what you feel in the moment in my book *The Emotional Compass: How To Think Better About Your Feelings* (Sand 2016b).

In the following section, we shall look at an example of how feelings may exist in layers and be difficult to distinguish from each other due to the self-protection strategy of regression.

Regression

When anxiety or fear becomes powerful enough, we sometimes resort to regression. Regression means that we fall back on the type of strategies that were a staple for an earlier stage of development. In regression, you feel small and helpless and, perhaps, furious like a hungry infant. Regression occurs when you are overwhelmed and give up your adult strategies. This is a path away from reality. We flee from the fact that we are grown people with responsibilities and options, and we forget momentarily everything we know how to do. The body language that accompanies regression, for example, may be that you slide down in your chair (become lower) and get tears in your eyes (call for help). Or we go to bed and stay there even though it is the middle of the day.

Iris is an example of how feelings exist in layers. She cried a lot when she was in therapy. But her tears were not especially deep. It did not seem as though there was any release in them. On the contrary, I got a sense of distance every time it happened. You might think that she was getting close to a genuine sorrow, but her weeping proved to be a sort of regression. Beneath the regression, there was anger and, beneath the anger, a sorrow with a completely different sort of depth.

Later, she described it this way:

When I resorted to regression, I cried sometimes for days. It was as if I fell into a deep despair and helplessness. At the same time, I felt a powerful anger toward the person or persons I thought should be there for me but weren't. When I came back to myself, I took a different tack and began to act and immediately felt better even though I was a little embarrassed when I looked in hindsight at my own reaction.

When people like Iris tip over into regression, a pervasive change occurs in the way they function in the world. Your adult 'ego' gives up control entirely or partially. In a way, everything becomes simpler and easier, more black and white and less nuanced. When you regress, those closest to you often wind up dealing with the problem.

Regression lasts for a few moments or an entire lifetime. The way out of regression is to remind yourself that childhood is over and that life is no longer so dangerous. Adults can survive for decades on a desert island. So, being scorned or excluded is no longer life threatening. As an adult, you can take new choices, and you have different options. If you cannot see any appropriate way out or a solution to the problem, you always have the possibility of seeking relevant professional help.

Chapter 7

DISMANTLING INAPPROPRIATE SELF-PROTECTION STRATEGIES

Once a self-protection strategy is revealed, it most often ceases to work automatically. Its secret power lies precisely in the fact that it is unconscious. If you realise that you are pulling the wool over your own eyes with the help of a self-protection strategy, the strategy loses its effect at that moment.

Then follows a period in which people experience pain and, sometimes, also joy more intensely. It may be connected with confusion and discomfort, and they may feel a bit like they are lost in the woods. Most people feel as if they have hiked out too far into the forest. But it may be that they have actually wandered into the woods from a place even farther out.

As you read this book, you will probably become aware of your own self-protection strategies and discover that you are getting closer to your own pain. Sometimes, however, it happens that the owner of a self-protection strategy is the last person to see it. Sometimes, we need help from the outside before we can become aware of what it is we do with ourselves in the moment.

Over the course of therapy, you borrow the attentiveness of the therapist. So, there are two of you looking at your strategies in life. In addition, I often encourage my clients to record our conversations on tape or video. This is a fantastic opportunity we have today to see ourselves from the outside, and assess whether what we are doing in the moment seems good or bad.

This is a way of heightening your attention that you can also use outside of therapy. If you record a video of a conflict you often have with a particular person, you can study the video together with the person in question. Probably, it will open the eyes of both parties.

In psychotherapy, there is a focus on how you handle yourself and your inner life. Some schools of thought focus more on self-protection strategies than others. But even in a therapy without a special focus on them, you may find that they lose strength as you become more secure and more in touch with yourself.

Let us say that Martin, whose mother was not able to deal with and validate him (Chapter 2), has now become a grown man. He has sought out therapy because his wife complains that she is having a hard time getting close to him.

If the therapist uses a form of therapy focusing on self-protection strategies, he will focus on perceiving what forms of self-protection Martin uses. He will tell Martin what he sees in the moment and, gradually, as Martin becomes aware of his strategies, they will lose their power.

The following dialogue is from a psychotherapeutic session in which the therapist uses the form of therapy known as 'intensive short-term dynamic psychotherapy' – a form of therapy that focuses on self-protection strategies.

Therapist (T): What do you want to do right now?

Martin (M): I don't know.

T: Have you noticed that you are almost not breathing?

(Impeding one's own breathing is an effective intrapsychic self-protection strategy, which we often do unconsciously when we are afraid that something may be painful.)

M: Oh, yeah. (takes a deep breath and breaks out in an unmotivated laughter)

T: You're laughing? What do you want to do right now?

M: (looks away)

T: Have you noticed that you are looking away? What do you feel right now?

M: (silence)

T: Your hands are clenched.

M: (silence)

T: Are you angry?

M: Maybe. (looks away)

The therapist knows that, when a self-protection strategy diminishes in strength, the next layer you meet is most often anger.

Above, we see how the first flicker of Martin's anger breaks through. His automatic self-protection strategies lose force more and more as they are revealed and articulated.

The therapist will ask Martin to describe his anger in all three components: his bodily experience, his understanding, and his impulse with a corresponding fantasy image. Optimally, it will ultimately be expressed directly to the therapist.

It might go like this:

Therapist (T): What are you feeling about me right now?

Martin (M): Irritation.

T: Can you feel it in your body?

M: My leg muscles are tight.

T: What do your legs want to do right now?

M: My right leg wants to kick your chair, so you fall over and tumble to the floor.

(Martin straightens up and takes a deep breath. Then, he looks directly at the therapist.)

T: How does my face look when I tumble to the floor?

M: You look sort of frightened.

(Martin's face lights up in a big smile, and the therapist sees a vitality he has not seen previously in Martin.)

When Martin begins to sense, get in touch with and express his genuine, primary feelings to the therapist, childhood memories will probably pop up. The situations that made self-protection strategies necessary suddenly come very close. They must be hauled into the light and worked through. All the feelings that were too overwhelming must be invited in, dealt with and expressed. It will be a great liberation for Martin to find that, now that he is an adult and together with another adult he feels safe with, he can deal with feelings that were unbearable in childhood.

Having your self-protection strategies described as they are going on is not an agreeable experience. Clients typically say it is extremely unpleasant – like being exposed, losing control and not knowing what to do.

A client who had entered into intensive short-term dynamic psychotherapy said after a session:

> In a way, this is both the best and the worst thing I've ever experienced. The worst because I felt totally insecure and helpless along the way. And the best because it gave me the experience of another person insisting on being close to me and not letting me slip away, who just kept on and on.

When you are in the process of dismantling a self-protection strategy, the protection mechanisms that are turned toward your surroundings will be the first thing to turn up – and they will typically appear in relation to the therapist. When their power diminishes, the client will probably be irritated at the therapist. What feelings may turn up first may vary, but it is most often anger.

Beneath the anger are other layers that will begin to appear as the process gradually moves forward.

A direct confrontation with self-protection strategies, as shown in the example above, is not good for everyone. But, for some, it can be very effective if used at the right point in time.

For others, it is better to use a form of therapy that is more cautious, one that, first and foremost, helps clients become better at sensing and understanding themselves. Self-protection strategies may sometimes dissolve by themselves when they are no longer necessary in the same way that a scab falls off a wound when the skin beneath has healed sufficiently.

I sometimes ask cautiously whether the client believes that a given way of thinking or behaving might be a self-protection strategy to create some distance from deeper feelings. If she clearly says no, I do not press more but think that either I am wrong or, to keep up the metaphor, the skin beneath is not yet ready to be exposed.

Some people dismantle their superfluous self-protection strategies without professional support – on their own or with the helpful attention of partners or, perhaps, friends. However, in most cases, it can be good to have a therapist or some other guide along the way – a person they feel safe with and can give them affirmation and inspire hope if the sorrow sometimes becomes too much.

Irritation and anger as self-protection

When an automatic self-protection technique is exposed, the person will typically react with irritation or anger. When Martin's self-protection strategies began to grow thin, he became angry with the therapist. Many of us may have a tendency to react with irritation or anger when others get close to us – even when what they are offering is something nice, something we would like.

Here's one example.

Helen was a client who was always unsatisfied with her relationships. One day, she told me that there was something that she was wondering about: there was a man, peripheral in her network, who had on several occasions suggested that they see each other, but she had declined. For some reason or other, she was terribly irritated at him – without understanding why. We investigated it more closely, and Helen began to formulate possible reasons for her irritation, for example, something about his attitudes she disagreed with. But none of the reasons could explain such a powerful reaction.

Only much later in the course of therapy did we find the explanation. An old, avoided grief popped up and, when it was worked through, Helen became much better at getting in touch with her own longing for concern from other people. And her irritation at the man disappeared. In fact, she subsequently had a great desire to be with him because she felt he could offer her more warmth and empathy than she was used to getting.

If you hide away a sorrow, a longing or a pain to which you have lost connection, being offered concern may give rise to mixed reactions. The 'forgotten' pain will push to come out and be cared for and give way to sorrow.

Sorrow is the path toward healing a wound. But since our psyche has an inherent need to avoid pain, we may have many self-protection strategies that – whether we are aware of it or not – block the path and keep us from getting close enough to the pain to grieve through it, from getting in touch with it and integrating it into our personality.

Our various self-protection strategies are in layers. Uppermost are the strategies that serve to protect us from our surroundings and, just beneath, are most often anger or irritation.

Anger is an effective form of self-protection both internally and externally: externally because it makes other people shut down and withdraw and internally because anger gladly takes the top layer, so you no longer feel the other emotions that might be there, for example powerlessness and sorrow.

And anger can easily be kept going by a swarm of thoughts that may have to do with feeling cheated or unfairly treated. People who have a tendency toward internal anger will typically have thoughts that circle around frustration and regret. It may be thoughts about how good everything could have been if they had acted differently – thoughts that they use to oppress themselves with. Internal anger can, like external anger, be a self-protection strategy against feeling more vulnerable emotions such as, for example, powerlessness, sorrow or, perhaps, a frail, forbidden joy.

If, as you are reading this book, you feel irritation, it may be because you are close to uncovering one of your own self-protection strategies – and you are using irritation to protect yourself from the confusion and discomfort that is the first step on the road to discovering a self-protection strategy and liberating yourself.

Anger is one of the layers in self-protection strategies – not the goal. Some people experience a great relief when the self-protection strategies that cover anger become so pliable that they can feel it more clearly than before. They discover that they become far better at saying 'no' and looking after themselves. And, consequently, they may well have the view that they have finally reached their goal.

But anger is a station on the way. It may be tempting to remain there and let anger move directly into behaviour.

Here is another example.

When Casper got in touch with his anger, he went home to his elderly parents and told them what he thought about the way they raised children and all the times he thought they had let him down. Getting everything out of his system gave him such relief that he was elated and had energy he had not felt in many years.

But letting anger move into behaviour in an unreflective way is a survival technique and not a constructive emotional skill. An outbreak of anger may lead to something positive and can, sometimes, be better than not expressing anything at all. And if you are good at asking for forgiveness, you can heal the relationship again if it has gotten any bruises.

For most people, however, it is best for everyone if you can contain your anger without immediately acting on it. It is best to wait on burdening others with it until you have done some internal work and accumulated the energy to contain your own anger and maintain empathy for and openness to the recipient.

Only many years later was Casper capable of seeing things from his parents' point of view. They had been taken unawares and were unhappy about his accusations, which they did not have wherewithal to understand. For a long time, they treated him with wariness and kept him at a distance because they were afraid of more abuse.

To feel and give expression to anger is not the ultimate goal. There is far more life in feeling and expressing the sorrow and longing that often lie just beneath the anger and can open the way to a greater experience of closeness and connectedness with other people.

Sorrow and pain

Beneath the self-protection strategies of irritation and anger is a layer of sorrow and pain. Some people believe that this is only true for people who have had a bad childhood. But no one has had perfect parents. When we were small, we have all felt disappointed, unloved or abandoned. And this has left its trace in us to a greater or lesser degree.

Let us continue the dialogue between Martin and the therapist. Some time has passed since Martin's anger broke through:

Therapist (T): What are you feeling in your body right now?

Martin (M): A lump in my throat, cold, sadness.

T: What are you missing?

M: Don't know. (looks away)

T: You're looking away, what do you feel?

M: Emptiness.

T: What is inside the emptiness?

M: (tears are flowing)

T: What do you want right now? Is there something I could say or do that would make you happy right now?

M: If you say you like me. (crying)

Then, a childhood memory pops up. Martin remembers how, at the dinner table, he watched his mother's face attentively as though he did not want to miss a rare chance to get a smile. His mother's face was most often closed and distant, and he remembers the experience of disappointment and loss when he left the table. Then, he could see himself as the cautious little boy he was – a boy who had tried his best to be loved but only received very little emotional closeness and attention. Here, Martin is feeling his own lack of love. It can be an earth-shattering experience to relive being unloved – especially when it involved people you were strongly connected with early in life. But that is the core of the problem, and it is the source for renewed vitality.

In commiseration with himself as a small boy and as the grown man he is today, someone who is still trying, he began to feel his sorrow.

When a self-protection strategy is cast off, feelings from childhood can suddenly appear with all their original intensity. At the beginning, it was very unpleasant for him when sorrow overwhelmed him; but, when he learned to accept it and make room for it, he discovered how close sorrow and joy are to each other and how life affirming it can be to allow both to be present. It is a matter of getting in touch with your sorrow. Give it room, put it into words, and integrate it, so it can be a part of our personality, so we can effortlessly own it and show it in close, safe relationships.

Many inappropriate patterns in life have come into being in an attempt to avoid sorrow and discomfort.

To be with yourself is also to be with the heartaches that have been in your life and with the love and lack of love you have encountered. If you have distanced yourself to feelings of love or lack of love from your childhood or later in life, you have probably distanced yourself from that place in yourself where you can feel whether or not other people like you.

Charlotte, who was in therapy for an extended period of time, says:

> Now that I've learned to feel whether the person I'm with likes me in his heart – or whether he just has an interest in getting together with me. If it is the latter, I invest less in the relationship and watch out for myself better.
>
> Once, I gave my whole heart to almost anyone who offered me a smile and a hand. Deep inside, I felt I was a wretched person who should be grateful if anyone deigned to be kind to me.
>
> After reliving episodes from my childhood, I can see now that I was once a loving child who lived under wretched conditions as far as emotional contact and warmth are concerned.
>
> At the start, this recognition was sometimes too overwhelming – even though the tears I shed were mostly from relief. It surged back and forth a bit for a time in which,

at one moment, I saw my new recognition in a clear light and, in the next moment, I harboured doubts about what I had just understood.

Now I have gradually cried my way through the chaos and the confusion I had to go through to find repose in a new identity, which has become my new foundation from which I decide what I want or do not want in a relationship with other people.

Charlotte's thought process – 'I am a wretched person' – had been buried deep inside her since childhood; and, no matter how much she tried positive thinking, it continued to pop up and control her field of attention and send her into depressive periods. It had the function of serving as a form of self-protection against feeling her lack of love in childhood. Not until Charlotte was able to look directly at the actual conditions under which she lived as a child and get in touch with her own emotional reaction to that reality did this tenacious, fundamental idea relax its grip on her, so she could find a new self-understanding that corresponded to her reality as a grown woman.

When you have dismantled the self-protection strategies that, today, do more harm than good, you will not necessarily feel happy. At first, you will probably feel vulnerable and exposed but, at the same time, experience an enhanced feeling of being alive. You will typically find that you are capable of being more present in your relationships for good or for ill. Some people say that they subsequently experience greater satisfaction and joy in successful relationships and, at the same time, greater pain in relationships in which closeness for one reason or another cannot be achieved.

The first time a person experiences being in touch with their own pain and, at the same time, being in good, close contact with another person, it feels powerfully life affirming.

Ursula relates:

> When I experienced being filled with a deep sorrow and, for the first time, did not have the urge to escape but remained in contact with my therapist, it was as if a whole new world opened up for me. I felt at once vulnerable and very alive. My view of what you can get out of this life expanded, and my hope and energy grew.

Many people use an incredible amount of energy to distance themselves from their own pain and other people. Integrating pain and allowing yourself to feel your sorrow and longing is the path to becoming free.

Figure 7.1 shows a graphic model of the various layers.

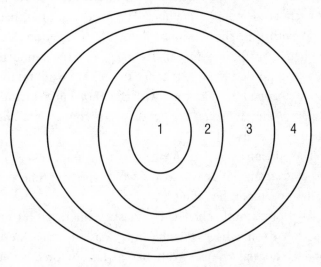

1. Love and connection   3. Irritation and anger

2. Sorrow and pain   4. Self-protection strategies

Figure 7.1 Layers of self-protection

Longing for love and contact

We are born ready to make close connections to other people. Just as birds instinctively know how to build a nest, a newborn infant is equipped with what is needed to create bonds.

A father and a mother each bring their own histories. They each come from a family and carry with them a social and biological heritage for good or ill. If a primary caregiver still lugs around major traumas in his or her baggage, there may be problems with bonding.

The child will later live with a powerful longing for something that he or she instinctively senses must exist but cannot see a clear image of.

Charlotte, whom we heard about in the last section, suddenly understood a recurring dream she had had for as far back as she could remember. The dream, in brief, had to do with this: she was in a life-or-death situation. She grabbed a telephone to call for help, but the numbers she was supposed to press to make the call were not on the phone's keypad. As she stood with the phone in her hand, desperate and in tears, trying to get a connection, she usually woke up.

The dream was an image of the loneliness and desperation she felt as a child and which she had, time and again, repeated in her adult life.

Charlotte's mother had had serious psychiatric problems, and it had only been possible for Charlotte to achieve good emotional contact with her in rare, unpredictable moments. As an adult, she had repeated a pattern in which she fell in love with fragile men whom she tried to help. Each time, she imagined that the man was deeply lonely and needed the contact she could offer. But the more she tried to give it to him, the more he withdrew. Each time, it ended in desperation and tears.

Over the course of therapy, Charlotte realised that the deep loneliness she sensed and tried to help men with was her own. She had tried to protect herself against her own loneliness and powerful yearnings by projecting them onto the men and by avoiding situations in which they were particularly strong. For long periods of time, she could not stand certain love songs; and, when one of her girlfriends fell in love, she withdrew from her.

Charlotte's loneliness and longing for love was just beneath her skin. She experienced it in powerful glimpses even though, for a long time, she could not bear to see its full extent; nor could she feel her own reaction at full strength. These glimpses had helped her not to become resigned but, instead, to keep looking for what she was missing. When she realised her pattern and processed her relationship with her mother and learned to get in touch with her own loneliness and longing, she no longer needed to avoid love songs and friends who were in love and other types of men began to turn up in her life.

Some people do not feel their longing for love. They content themselves with a meagre emotional life. They have given up the belief that more than that exists. Maybe they dope themselves with too much food, sleep, entertainment or other forms of regular abuse. But even for these people, their longing can appear in dreams and fantasies. Or it can stick its nose out as envy or contempt for those who live a life in which they make room for their feelings.

The people who can feel their longing – however painful it may be – are closer to finding what they long for than those who cannot.

Some people have stable relationships with family and friends and, perhaps, also a partner but have longings anyway. They probably need to learn to come closer. In my book *Highly Sensitive People in an Insensitive World* (Sand 2016a), you can read about how to move up and down in different layers of contact. It provides various tools for controlling how superficial or deep you want a given relationship to be.

When you learn something new about your own origins and about yourself, the question often arises whether you should share your new insight with those they are about.

The relationship with your parents today

When you begin to get a more realistic view of your parents and yourself, you are doing work on your inner self, a process that typically takes a long time. The extent to which it is good to burden your parents with your new insights may be different from relationship to relationship.

But it is important to be aware that, if you have lived with an idealised picture of your parents and it has shattered, it will probably tip over into devaluation for a period. From having seen them as better than they are or were, it is common to fall into the trap of seeing them as worse than they are or were.

One example is Maria, who was often heard to say: 'My parents have given me everything.' When her parental idealisation shattered, everything turned upside down. Now, she saw them as people who had given her nothing good. But, after some months, she began to find a balance and recalled episodes in which her parents had actually supported her in a genuine and unselfish way.

She followed her therapist's advice to wait to share these new insights with her parents until she was well settled inside her new way of looking at the world.

Another example is Sophia. She realises perfectly well that her mother probably did not act the way she did out of spite. She knew that her mother was the victim of her social and biological heritage. Nevertheless, Sophia was overwhelmed with disappointment when her idealisation fell apart. She felt her mother had cheated her; and, over the long run, it was too difficult for Sophia to grapple with her understanding of her mother and her own anger at the same time.

During that period, she limited her contact with her mother to emails since being face to face in a room with her spurred such anger and frustration in Sophia that it was too stressful and overwhelming.

After an extensive course of therapy, Sophia became capable of containing her disappointment and sorrow, so she could once again be together with her mother in an adult and composed way. Gradually, she also garnered the energy to acknowledge her mother for the attempts she made and for previously having made the effort to make contact with her daughter.

In the best case scenario, once one's view of Mum and Dad has been revised, a completely new and much more equal relationship between parents and their adult children can arise. In the worst case, parents cannot deal with their children viewing them differently – and it can happen that the relationship becomes so distressing that the best thing for all parties may be to cease contact. However, there are many possible middle roads between these two extremes. Settling on seeing each other for two hours twice a year may be a good solution to a difficult relationship that you nevertheless do not want to give up on altogether.

Changing your view of yourself and your parents is a radical process that, sometimes, surges back and forth between different extremes until you find a balance. One extreme is seeing your parents as better than they are. The other is seeing them as worse.

You can fall into the same extremes about yourself. For some periods, you see yourself as a fantastic personality while, in other periods, you see yourself as a loser. And your vision of your partner will often alternate with your vision of yourself, so that for a period you feel far too good for your partner or lover if you are single and want to go your own way – while, at another time, you do not think you can live up to your partner's expectations and are overwhelmed with anxiety at being abandoned.

The art of living is finding a balance. And this requires a certain capaciousness that, sometimes, must first be constructed before it can be realised. In order to find a foothold in the middle, you must dare to be yourself with the flaws and virtues you have.

Chapter 8

THE WAY HOME

Behind the social mask

When the fear of being anything but 'right' is sufficiently large, the social mask becomes inflexible. For some people, it hardens into a grimace they never entirely take off.

If you would like to see a face without the social mask, you can look into a bus that happens to pass by. You may be fortunate enough to catch sight of a passenger who is looking out the window, thinking he or she is unobserved. They will probably look very relaxed. Maybe their jaw droops or the corners of their mouth. But the moment someone speaks to that person, he or she will immediately pull their face together, put on the mask and, perhaps, smile.

It is good to have a social mask you can put on when you are navigating social spaces. It would be inappropriate to go around displaying an entirely open visage everywhere. The problem is if you yourself do not realise when you are putting your mask on or taking it off or if you never dare take it off – even in your closest relationships.

One client relates:

For many years, I couldn't fall asleep if a man was lying beside me. It was as if I didn't dare relax my face. Later, in therapy, I discovered what I was afraid of. I was simply afraid that the man would wake up in the middle of the night and see me sleeping. You can't fall asleep with a smile and count on it lasting the whole night through. I was afraid I would look repulsive when I was asleep and had to give up control over my face and that he would distance himself from me and leave me.

Showing your face as it is can be the way to good contact – and it is infectious. If you look into a face that is extremely relaxed and open, your own face will want to do the same. By the same token, if you see a face with a big smile, it suddenly becomes very hard not to smile – even if you are not at all happy.

Yet, a smile can prevent both the smiling person and the person being smiled at to sense themselves properly. For example, it can make it hard to say that you feel bad if the other person is smiling all the time. A smile that is more of a mask than an expression of a person's inner reality can be used as a self-protection strategy. An uninterrupted stream of chatter can do the same thing. It is very difficult to achieve authentic contact with a person who is always talking. On the other hand, if both parties dare to take a break from the stream of words, allow the social mask to fall, and make good eye contact, a life-affirming sense of closeness may arise.

Letting go of your social mask and allowing your face to fall into exactly the folds it wants because it reflects your inner reality at that moment can be frightening if this is something you only rarely or, perhaps, never do. But it is the way to better contact both internally and externally.

If you are to be authentically present in your own life in a way that allows you to feel you are alive, you have to let go of the struggle to be right or good or clever or whatever you want to be in your own eyes or the eyes of others. You must reach a point where you dare to be – without wanting to be something particular. The attitude of 'I am who I am' is a good, basic outlook that can give you room to contact and explore your own deeper feelings, desires or longings, so you can get a good sense of yourself from within.

Choosing to be yourself – in order to choose to encounter others

If we are to see and understand ourselves clearly, there must not be too many unconscious, automatic self-protection strategies going on. They veil our vision and keep us from being able to sense our inner selves and other people on their own premises.

Choosing to be yourself is deciding to work to get in touch with your own inner reality and to stand by yourself even when you are not able to live up to your own or others' ideals.

It is also accepting that we do not have power over most of what really means something in life. Choosing to be yourself is an exercise in letting go of control and going with the stream of life.

Life is movement. We are ourselves in constant change. The people we connect with we must one day let go again. Life alternates between sorrow and wonder.

The person who dares to be a human being on these conditions, and can accept being the person he is, can act from what he senses in the now and does not need to be controlled by what he once sensed and was afraid of. And, thus, present in the now, he can encounter others. In order to be able to experience a genuine encounter in the now, both people must dare to be themselves.

We can be together without having a genuine encounter. For example, we can be together in a consumption mode. Maybe we use other people as a diversion, for entertainment, to get information, recognition or whatever we are after. People can use each other the way they use objects. Instead of turning on the television and getting entertainment in that way, you can call a friend and gossip for a while. It is not at all certain that you are interested in having a genuine encounter. Maybe you do not have the energy for deeper social contact at the moment or maybe you do not have much interest in the other person's inner life.

There is nothing wrong with using each other in this way every so often. If we were to be in full contact with ourselves and each other all the time, life would be far too strenuous. But it produces a lower quality of life if this form of contact is the only one we offer or receive – or if we ourselves do not realise what is what.

In a genuine encounter, there is no agenda. There is no determinate goal, nothing you want out of it, nothing you are going to use the other person for. In a genuine encounter, you relate to each other in the moment that is. What happens is unpredictable, and you risk being changed by the encounter. Maybe a powerful moment arises with a feeling that 'I know that you know that I know' or 'I feel that you feel that I feel'.

Feeling loved is feeling that you are seen and accepted exactly as you are. To be able to love, among other things, is to be able to see, to adjust, and to accept yourself and others.

'All actual life is encounter', says the Jewish philosopher Martin Buber (2010). We cannot plan or decide on an encounter of such a high quality, one in which we really feel we are really living. But we can create the best preconditions for it. And that is exactly what we are doing when we examine our self-protection strategies and choose to stand by ourselves. When we do that, new possibilities open up for relationships, and everything becomes simpler.

Letting go of the struggle to be good enough – and other bad investments

If you have invested a lot of energy in being good enough – and, for most people, this means good enough to be sure of being loved – it is difficult to throw in the towel and give up an impossible project, especially if it has been going on for many years.

It can be compared to having invested a lot of money on shares in a company that promised smooth sailing for the rest of your life. When you are just about to lose hope, you learn that you have to invest even more for it to be successful.

The day you choose to turn off the stream of money (stream of energy) from your pocket and into the company's, you can realise that you made a bad investment. This may unleash sorrow over the life you have wasted on this account. If, on the other hand, you just keep investing more and more in the hope that the impossible will one day be possible, you can avoid this unpleasant truth and your own grief.

A recognition that the strategies and rules by which you have guided your life have not led to the desired result, and never will, can be both shocking and overwhelming. Just discovering that there are other ways of living that are more satisfactory can unleash sorrow – even though it is, at the same time, the path toward a more satisfactory life and greater happiness.

Here is an example.

Anne had children early and decided to remain a housewife. Even though her life was often lonely and boring, she did not think she could handle being out among people eight hours a day.

When, for the first time as a 35-year-old, she had to get a job for economic reasons, she discovered that she was energised by being out among people, and her mood rose to such a level that she almost could not recognise herself. She had been a housewife for 15 years and had a hard time dealing with her new recognition that she was doing much better by going to work. In order to protect herself against this, she harboured doubts about it for a long time. She told herself that it was probably only the newness of it all that made it interesting and gave her this surprising joy. But, gradually, she let the recognition sink in that she could handle going to work and that it gave her new energy that also benefited her children.

In the long run, her new happiness exceeded by far the sorrow that had accumulated over 15 lonely years. But, right at first, the sorrow was overwhelming. And if you are not good at grieving or have avoided sorrows in your life, it can be tempting to return to the old pattern and sow doubt about your new happiness, which you try to tone down or forget entirely.

Here, I think the reason is that many people hang onto old patterns and obsolete strategies and are only able to find release and grieve themselves free when or if they are fortunate enough to be hit by a crisis or some other opportunity for growth.

If you have a major sorrow that you have avoided dealing with or have not worked through, you may be just as sensitive to new sorrows as people with PTSD (Post-Traumatic Stress Disorder) are to reliving their trauma.

Fortunately, in our time, there are many opportunities to seek professional help to work through old traumas and to learn to get in touch with yourself and the uncertainties of life.

If you would like to live life awake and present in sorrow and joy, you have to be good at letting go. You have to be able to say good-bye to people and things to which you are connected, so you can accept the new that appears ahead. Life is movement. We meet and form bonds. We part and must grieve ourselves free in order to start all over again in new relationships. There are times to cry and times to laugh. We have no control over most of what can arouse the greatest joy or the deepest sorrow. But if you are good at letting go and grieving yourself free, you are well equipped for life's hardships.

Crisis as a step along the way

When the reality and self-understanding that have been self-evident to you are questioned, it can give rise to a form of crisis.

When Anne realised that her husband actually cared more about her than she thought and that the negative picture she had of him said more about herself than him, she lost her foothold and, for a period, she was in doubt about everything she had thought and believed before. She described it herself as being out in deep water, and many months went by before she could find herself again in a new way.

She later said:

Before I became aware of my self-protection strategies, my self-assurance was greater than it is today. At that time, I experienced myself as well functioning and was just annoyed that, again and again, I ran into people who were enormously difficult to be with. To discover that I was actually the person who generated some of that difficulty was really unpleasant.

Sometimes, life feels easier before you begin to look at yourself. But it is also more impoverished. The worse you know and understand yourself, the poorer is the quality of your relationships with other people. If you cannot see others or yourself clearly, complications will arise time and again, and it will be difficult to understand or feel yourself understood in your relationships. And the less you feel and understand yourself, the more indistinct will be your experience of being alive.

Life-altering pain – when we come closer to our inner selves

Many accounts can be found about how people who have a life-threatening disease take their entire lives up for review and change it in a positive direction. Afterwards, they often exclaim, 'Why didn't I realise much earlier that this change could bring more happiness into my life and those close to me?'

One of the answers is that we are creatures of habit. If we are not subjected to a sufficient amount of pressure, we keep going down the same track we are familiar with and are comfortable with.

Getting closer to reality, which you do when you cast off inappropriate self-protection strategies, can have the same effect as a serious illness: we find motivation to change ourselves even though it can be frightening. Sometimes, the pain in our lives has to reach a certain level before we cast off secure and convenient habits and throw ourselves into something new.

When Dorothy got closer to her reality, she understood at a deeper level that she had missed out on some of the best things in life because she never dared to dive deeply into a loving relationship. And it was clear to her that the time she had to fix things was limited since she was already past midlife. This insight threw her into a crisis that led to a tremendous grief.

She had to take antidepressants before she found the energy to change her life. Then, she did something she had always sworn she would never do: she created a profile on a dating site. Here, she discovered that it was personally developing for her to put into words what she could and would offer a prospective partner – and, particularly, what her own desires were. Later, she discovered that she found it interesting and inspiring to go on dates. When she stopped therapy, she had not yet found a boyfriend, but she had met a man who had become an important friend.

Susanne had kept her inner self at an appropriate distance her whole life by always being three steps ahead of herself. She was always obsessed with what was going to happen in a bit, tomorrow or next year. Her head was completely preoccupied with planning and thoughts about how good it was all going to be when she was finished with everything she was working on.

When she dropped this self-protection, she felt the pain in her life as it was in the moment. She had not been intimate with her husband for the last 10 years or more. The reason was that she was angry at him for reasons that she could now see had to do with the fact that she could not stand her own life.

When Susanne looked closely at this reality, she went into a deep sorrow that, for many years, she had neglected her love life and had blamed her husband for things that he realistically had nothing to do with nor could he do anything about. Her grief might resemble a depression, and she received good advice from some of her friends not to think so negatively and, instead, focus on the positive. But the truth was that Susanne was now thinking more realistically and was closer to reality than she had ever been before. In the midst of her sorrow, she stretched her arms out toward her husband and could, as something entirely new, accept without reservation all the care he offered her.

The motivation to change old patterns grows out of pain and frustration over an unlived life. When we stop drowning unpleasantness in too much food, entertainment, too much sleep, intoxicants or other self-protection strategies, it is allowed to grow sufficiently large, so that we realise that we must change.

Casting off unnecessary self-protection strategies is the beginning of a new way to be present in life. The first step is to pay attention to ourselves, to review our own strategies in life and investigate whether that particular strategy serves to develop our lives or whether it obscures our knowledge and muddles our relationships.

Awareness is the way forward

If we do not all live in vital and developing love relationships, it is due, among other things, to the fact that many people need to be better at getting close to themselves and others – so close that they can see themselves and the other person clearly. Then, encounters of a high quality may arise.

The way out of the labyrinth of self-protection strategies is awareness. The less conscious we are about our own inner selves, the more things can run in circles or lead us around by the nose without us realising what is really going on.

Simply knowing that unconscious self-protection strategies exist increases our focus and improves our ability to see our own strategies.

This interest in our inner selves, that many of us did not have enough of when we were children, can be cultivated in ourselves as adults. Instead of remaining stuck in the same patterns, we can inspect our own strategies and take a position on which of them can profitably be adjusted or dismantled entirely.

With an open, unbiased and accommodating awareness and interest in ourselves, we can develop a capaciousness to the diversity of life we have within us. And with this capaciousness and the courage to be ourselves, we can offer an equally open and accepting attention to other people.

Through the personal work described above, the best prerequisites are present in order for us to feel our own vitality and connect in love.

THANKS TO

MSc in Psychology and head of the Institute for Gestalt Analysis Niels Hoffmeyer, with whom I studied intensive short-term dynamic therapy, and registered psychotherapist and theologist Bent Falk, with whom I studied gestalt therapy.

I must also thank all of you who, over time, have shown me confidence in sharing your thoughts and feelings – whether it was at the rectory, in my therapeutic practice, at my lectures or elsewhere. A special thanks to those of you who gave me permission to use your stories in this book.

Thanks, too, to those of you who have read my manuscript and given me feedback. Without the back and forth I had with you, the book would not be nearly as good. I would like to mention here: Martin Håstrup, Janet Cecilie Ligaard, Jens Rasmussen, Kirstine Sand and Pia Skadhede. You have each in your way placed your imprint on this book.

Bibliography

Buber, Martin (2010) *I and Thou*. Eastford, CT: Martino Fine Books.

Davanloo, Habib (1978) *Basic Principles and Techniques in Short-Term Dynamic Psychotherapy*. New York: Spectrum Publications.

Davanloo, Habib (1990) *Unlocking the Unconscious*. New York: Wiley.

Davidsen-Nielsen, Marianne and Leick, Nini (1991) *Healing Pain: Attachment, Loss, and Grief Therapy*. London: Routledge.

Della Selva, Patricia Coughlin (1996) *Intensive Short-term Dynamic Psychotherapy: Theory and Technique*. London: Karnac Books.

Freud, Sigmund (1926) *Inhibitions, Symptoms and Anxiety*. Eastford, CT: Martino Fine Books.

Jung, C.G. (1964) *The Undiscovered Self. Civilization in Transition (Collected Works of C.G. Jung)*. London: Routledge.

Kierkegaard, Søren (1981) *The Concept of Anxiety*. Princeton, NJ: Princeton University Press; first edition (US).

Kierkegaard, Søren (1989) *The Sickness Unto Death*. London: Penguin Classics.

Miller, Alice (1997) *The Drama of the Gifted Child*. New York: Basic Books.

O'Toole, Donna (1988) *Aarvy Aardvark Finds Hope*. Burnsville, NC: Compassion Press.

Sand, Ilse (2016a) *Highly Sensitive People in an Insensitive World: How to Create a Happy Life*. London: Jessica Kingsley Publishers.

Sand, Ilse (2016b) *The Emotional Compass: How to Think Better About Your Feelings.* London: Jessica Kingsley Publishers.

Yalom, Irvin D. (1980) *Existential Psychotherapy.* New York: Basic Books.

Young, Jeffrey E. (1990) *Cognitive Therapy for Personality Disorders: A Schema-Focused Approach.* Portland, OR: Professional Resource Exchange Inc.